How to
Treat
NEW
Ideas

This series of books draws on the practical knowledge that the Center for Creative Leadership (CCL®) has generated, since its inception in 1970, through its research and educational activity conducted in partnership with hundreds of thousands of managers and executives. Much of this knowledge is shared—in a way that is distinct from the typical university department, professional association, or consultancy. CCL is not simply a collection of individual experts, although the individual credentials of its staff are impressive; rather it is a community, with its members holding certain principles in common and working together to understand and generate practical responses to today's leadership and organizational challenges.

The purpose of the series is to provide managers with specific advice on how to complete a developmental task or solve a leadership challenge. In doing that, the series carries out CCL's mission to advance the understanding, practice, and development of leadership for the benefit of society worldwide. We think you will find the Ideas Into Action Series an important addition to your leadership toolkit.

How to
Treat
NEW
Ideas

David Magellan Horth
Michael T. Mitchell

Center for
Creative
Leadership

IDEAS INTO ACTION SERIES

Aimed at managers and executives who are concerned with their own and others' development, each book in this series gives specific advice on how to complete a developmental task or solve a leadership problem.

LEAD CONTRIBUTORS
David Magellan Horth, Michael T. Mitchell

CONTRIBUTORS
George Hallenbeck

DIRECTOR, PEOPLE, PROCESS, AND PROJECTS
Davida Sharpe

MANAGER, PUBLICATION DEVELOPMENT
Peter Scisco

ASSOCIATE EDITOR
Shaun Martin

WRITER
Linda Edgerton

DESIGN, LAYOUT, AND COVER DESIGN
Ed Morgan, navybluedesign.com

RIGHTS AND PERMISSIONS
Kelly Lombardino

EDITORIAL BOARD
David Altman, Elaine Biech, Regina Eckert, Joan Gurvis, Jennifer Habig, Kevin Liu, Neal Maillet, Jennifer Martineau, Portia Mount, Laura Santana

CCL No. 00468

978-1-60491-761-1 – Print
978-1-60491-762-8 – Ebook

Center for Creative Leadership
www.ccl.org

Cover photo: Evan Kirby erkirby.com
Intro page photo: Luke Carliff

Contents

Handle with Care:

How to Give New Ideas the Respect They Deserve

New ideas are the lifeblood of an organization. They fuel innovation and initiatives that can benefit your customers and stakeholders. They can promote growth and help you capture new market share. They also can inspire members of your team and keep them energized, engaged, and excited about your organization's prospects.

But new ideas are also fragile things. Depending on how you and other leaders in your organization handle new ideas, they can be snuffed out in the blink of an eye. This dismissal may seem surprising, since most of us say we value innovation and want our team members to be creative. But when faced with the reality of a new idea, our actions often prove otherwise. Rather than examining new ideas carefully and nurturing those that hold promise, we are more likely to simply kill them before they get out of the gate.

Why? It is easy to get spooked by the strangeness of new ideas. They can seem ambiguous and risky. As a result, we criticize rather than praise and dismiss new ideas instead of giving them a fair shot—stifling innovation in the process.

In fairness, few of us have been taught what to do when new ideas come along. Instead, we are schooled in the nuts and bolts of management. We learn how to stay the course and make incremental quality improvements. In addition, the organizations we work for typically don't reward us for nurturing innovation. Instead, we are recognized and acknowledged for work based on proven, time-tested precedents that seem safe and risk-free.

One example: Some years ago, CCL visited a company to discuss ways to promote innovation. One of the individuals we interviewed was a director of software development who was a people person and beloved by his team. When we asked him

"What do you do when someone comes to you with a new idea?"

he thought for a few moments and responded: "I tell them to take the afternoon off." Intrigued by his answer, we asked why, thinking perhaps he was using time away as a reward for those coming up with new ideas. We were astonished when he said instead that he gave team members time off in hopes that the ideas they had proposed would go away.

While our first reaction to radical new ideas may be to wish they would go away, dismissing them can mean the loss of incredible new opportunities. One example is found in the experiences of innovator Steve Wozniak. In an interview with Britain's *The Telegraph*, Wozniak says he initially proposed the idea of a personal computer to his bosses at Hewlett-Packard. Company executives are reported to have repeatedly dismissed the idea—not once, not twice, but "no less than five times." After all, why would ordinary people need a computer of their own? Unlike many innovators, however, Wozniak was persistent. He joined Steve Jobs in founding Apple Computer and in bringing the PC to life, a decision that has transformed our world in countless ways.

Though the Wozniak example is dramatic, leaders in organizations around the globe make the same short-sighted decisions about all types of new ideas. If we are to foster innovation, change is needed. And it must begin at the personal level. Leaders need to develop an awareness of the personal reactions and behaviors that can kill fragile new ideas before they have a chance to blossom. It takes a bit of skill and lots of purposeful practice.

By understanding why we react to new ideas the way we do, we can learn to encourage, nurture, and protect them from the start. We can ensure new ideas get a fair shot and are carefully considered to determine whether they have potential.

In the text that follows, you'll find out how you can break the mold and be poised to do great things with the new ideas that come your way. We offer six specific tips and techniques you can use to encourage new ideas, push and pull them in new directions, build on their potential, and turn them into something truly innovative.

FOOD for *thought*

Think about a time you had a new and creative idea that you shared with your boss or someone else in your organization. Perhaps it was an idea for a new product or service, a new way of connecting to your customers, a suggestion about changing an internal process, or about partnering with another organization.

How was the idea received? What happened when the idea was shared with your boss or colleagues? How open and receptive were they? What kinds of comments were made? How did you feel afterwards?

The Innovation Leadership Gap

When CCL surveyed global executives about the importance of innovation, 94% said innovation is important or very important to organizational success. When we asked the same executives if their organization is effective at innovation, the number dropped to just 14%. That's a striking gap between the importance of innovation and an organization's ability to consider and nurture new ideas to determine whether they hold promise.

When we asked executives what actions organizations could take to improve innovation, the top two responses were:

- Build a culture that supports innovation.
- Develop leaders that encourage innovation.

Developing your own skills in innovation leadership can be an important first step in helping your organization develop a culture of innovation.

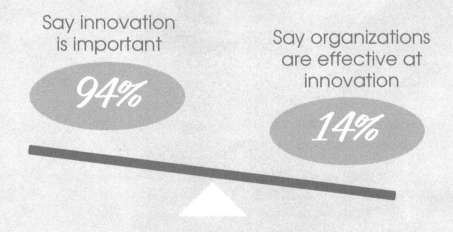

Say innovation is important

94%

Say organizations are effective at innovation

14%

Tip 1

Resist the Instinct to Kill a New Idea

CCL research shows that self-awareness is a critical competency for any leader and a key determiner of how effective you will be throughout your career. That's especially true when it comes to nurturing new ideas. If you want to embrace innovation, it's important to recognize what your likely first response will be when you are faced with a proposal that is new and innovative.

For most of us, like it or not, our first instinct will be to kill the new idea out of hand, without stopping to give it proper consideration. When we try to align a new idea into our existing mental framework, we notice the sharp edges. We focus on what doesn't fit instead of what does. Rather than embracing and nurturing the idea, we see it as a threat that we run away from or try to neutralize. That's because new ideas challenge us in three important ways.

Threat 1

New Ideas Are Risky

By their very nature, new ideas are unproven. They might work, or they might not, and that means risk. As we rise through the leadership ranks, most of us are trained to eliminate risk and to avoid any moves that gamble the future of our organization on the unknown. As a result, we instinctively want to avoid the risk a new idea represents.

CCL's experience with a senior marketing director for a large global organization says it all. When we asked him how he responded when people came to him with new ideas, he had an immediate and dramatic answer. "If 100 people in this organization came to me with new ideas, I would have to fire every one of them," he said. "Unfortunately, another 100 people with ideas would stand up, and I would have to fire them too. Why can't people just do what they have been asked and support the company strategy?"

In this leader's mind, new ideas that might challenge the established company strategy were a threat to be eliminated, and he was just the guy to do it. What boundless opportunities must he have missed as a result.

Threat 2

New Ideas Can Challenge Power Structures

When a new idea takes hold, it can have a ripple effect. It can take individuals, departments, and organizations in a new direction, which opens the door for new power brokers to emerge. Those currently in power may lose influence or be forced to step aside completely.

Let's say you work for a consumer products company. As ideas for new products emerge and become popular, the demand for existing brands may decline. That will likely trigger a drop in funding for existing products. Those in charge of the older brands may find they are no longer as valuable or influential in the company. Instead, the power structure shifts to those who control new brands.

If you've watched this happen to colleagues, what do you think your reaction would be when an idea for a new brand is presented? Would you embrace the new idea and nurture it along in a way that will benefit the broader organization? Or would you instead feel threatened and do your best to torpedo the new idea right out of the gate?

Threat 3

New Ideas Are Most Often Not Our Own

As human beings, many of us tend to fall victim to the well-known "not invented here" syndrome. We simply reject ideas that come from someone else. Perhaps we believe the idea won't work because the person who came up with it doesn't have the experience we do. Perhaps we resent not coming up with the idea ourselves. Whatever the case, this gut reaction can damage our objectivity and thus ability to evaluate a new idea.

Effective leaders find ways to break the pattern. They understand that most ideas will not be their own and can bubble up from anyone and anywhere in the organization. Rather than shouldering the sole responsibility for dreaming up new innovations, it is a leader's role to encourage the new ideas we encounter, evaluate them fairly, and build on their potential.

Using Self-Awareness to Break the Pattern

Understanding how your brain works can be a big help in developing the self-awareness you need to embrace new ideas and give them a fair shot. When we are faced with information that threatens our status quo, our natural tendency is to either fight it off tooth and nail or distance ourselves from the threat.

This "fight or flight" response is hardwired into our limbic system—a very large and well-developed part of the brain. When the limbic system senses a threat and reacts, it can swamp the reactions of the much smaller prefrontal cortex—the "executive judgment" center that is typically in charge as you make decisions and move through your day.

Let's say you are riding an elephant and guiding it using reins, but the elephant suddenly gets spooked and charges forward on its own, ignoring the reins entirely. That's how your brain operates. Most of the time the rational, cognitive part of your brain is in control. But when a perceived threat emerges, the limbic system takes charge and gallops around wherever it wants. New ideas and the threat they represent can trigger the elephant to take charge.

Rather than reasoning through what's good and what's bad about a new idea, we simply kill it and move on.

To break the pattern, we need to slow down, become more mindful, and pay attention to our responses. This self-awareness is essential to making sense of a situation and to understanding why we're reacting in the way that we are. Rather than giving in to the "fight or flight" instincts that are our natural, neurological response, we can take a deep breath, reassess the situation, and moderate the rampaging elephant.

9

This "slowing down" to notice and understand your reactions can be hard unless you have a fair degree of self-awareness. Without it, in many ways you are living in a protective bubble that insulates you from ideas, actions, and beliefs that challenge the status quo and your own preconceived notions of the world.

The bubble shields you from criticism and accountability for mistakes, and it keeps you from developing an accurate understanding of your strengths and your limitations.

You are thus unlikely to recognize your "fight or flight" instinct when it kicks in, making it impossible for you to give new ideas proper consideration.

Leaders who are self-aware know who they are, what they are reasonably capable of, what their weaknesses are, how their behavior affects others, and how others see them. Self-aware leaders may still inhabit a bubble where they retreat during particularly stressful times, but it is relatively thin, transparent, and permeable. They can confidently take in new information and ideas that their less self-aware counterparts might consider a threat. They are able to recognize their destructive tendencies, rise above them, and make sound choices that benefit themselves and the team they lead. As a result, they are less likely to flee from new ideas or to derail them right out of the gate.

Exercise

Conquering the "Fight or Flight" Response

Are you truly aware of how you react to new ideas? Try this exercise to help you become more attuned to your responses:

- Close your eyes and think of a new idea you've encountered at work or in your personal life that seemed risky to you.

- Focus on those risks and notice your physical reaction. Does the very notion of the new idea cause your mind to race, your breathing to become heavier, or your heart to beat at a higher than normal rate? Are you experiencing numbness or tingling from the surge of adrenaline?

- Now, take a breath and imagine the possible positive outcomes if the idea were to be fully and successfully executed. As you envision this more positive future, notice your physical reaction. Is your mind more focused? Are your breathing and heart rate more normal? Are you experiencing less numbness and tingling?

- Try this same refocusing exercise as you encounter other new ideas. With practice, you can "change tracks" in your mind, think of new ideas more positively, and begin to embrace the possibilities they might represent.

11

Tip 2
Practice Innovation Thinking

In the workplace, most of us seek to remove ambiguity, make quick decisions, and drive immediate results. We look for research, logical facts, proof, and precedent to inform and guide the important decisions we make. We use this information to tease out the right answer from among all the wrong answers in front of us. Whether an idea is *feasible* becomes much more important to us than whether it represents a creative new breakthrough.

Our CCL colleagues did some research recently around feasibility and creativity. They spoke to business leaders and their customers to determine which of a series of new product ideas each liked the best. They found that the best predictor of which products customers were most likely to buy was how creative the ideas behind them were. When our colleagues showed the same ideas to business leaders, though, those leaders were attracted to the ideas that seemed most feasible and much less interesting to customers.

The logical, fact-based approach and focus on feasibility that characterizes business thinking can be important to organizational success. But business thinking can easily kill a transformative new idea before it has a chance to be fully considered. That's why great leaders also practice innovation thinking.

Unlike business thinking, innovation thinking doesn't rely on past experience or known facts. It involves imagining a desired future state and how you might get there. It is about being intuitive and remaining open to possibility. Rather than identifying right answers or wrong answers, the goal is to explore possibilities. Ambiguity becomes an advantage, not a problem. It allows us to ask "What if?" and to find a better path forward.

Managing the tension between these two seemingly opposite ways of thinking is not about discarding one method in favor of the other. Instead, it's about acknowledging that both exist and that finding productive new products and services will result from the right balance between the two approaches. The most talented leaders are able to switch seamlessly between these two ways of seeing the world. They begin by adopting innovation thinking when evaluating new ideas and exploring their potential. They ask,

"What is unique about the idea, and what might we do with it? How might it benefit our customers and stakeholders? Could we build on the idea to make it even stronger and more compelling?"

These leaders switch to business thinking when they are ready to make decisions about how they will bring a new idea to life and sustain it over time. Their questions become more specific and process-based. "What will our timeline be for bringing the idea to market? What budget resources and staff will we need? Do we need to build new supporting systems? How will we gather customer feedback and ensure we respond to it effectively?"

Both ways of thinking are fundamental to leadership success. The key is to make certain that you don't let business thinking take over when you first encounter a new idea, and that you don't rely solely on innovation thinking as you begin to build the supporting infrastructure to launch your new idea once it is fully formed.

Business Thinking vs. Innovation Thinking

Business Thinking	Innovation Thinking
Logical	Intuitive
Deductive/Inductive reasoning	Abductive reasoning
Requires proof to proceed	Asks "What if?"
Looks for precedents	Unconstrained by the past
Quick to decide	Holds multiple possibilities
There is right and wrong	There is always a better way
Uncomfortable with ambiguity	Relishes ambiguity
Wants results	Wants meaning

FOOD for *thought*

Consider the following questions. Evaluate your responses and think through what kind of changes you might make to become a more effective leader of innovation by utilizing both business and innovation thinking.

- What type of thinking do you most often use as you exercise leadership?

- Do you find yourself supporting creative ideas? Or do you endorse only those ideas that you know right away can be made to work?

- When you or a member of your team begins to worry about feasibility issues while an idea is still at the consideration stage, how might you break the cycle? What questions could you ask to reframe the discussion and focus on the possibilities?

Tip 3
Frame and Clarify the Idea's Purpose

Once you've overcome your natural tendency to kill an idea based on the threat it represents or how hard you think it will be to implement, it's time to begin taking a close look at what the idea is all about.

One important next step is to frame the idea by identifying what problem it might solve or what opportunity it might address. Are there customer needs or complaints that the new idea might resolve? Could it help your organization operate more efficiently or take advantage of new market opportunities? Understanding the possibilities an idea represents will give it a much better chance of taking root and thriving as it moves through your organization. By framing and giving the idea purpose, it no longer seems so crazy or random.

One famous example of the importance of purpose is found in the story behind the invention of the Post-it Note. Back in the 60s, 3M scientist Spencer Silver set out to develop a super-strong adhesive. He didn't get the outcome he expected. Instead of super-strong properties, he got an adhesive that was "low-tack" and pressure-sensitive, making it able to be detached and reused. It was the opposite of what he thought a great adhesive was supposed to do, which was to hold firmly and permanently.

At the time, Silver couldn't find any useful purpose for his invention, and it lingered on the shelf. The breakthrough came as he talked with his colleague Art Fry, who was a member of a church choir. Fry had been using slips of paper to mark the day's hymns in his hymnal, allowing him to quickly turn to the right page and sing his part. But he was having a problem keeping the strips of paper from falling out. He wondered whether Silver's low-tack adhesive might be the perfect solution to his need—helping him reliably bookmark each week's songs in his hymnal. Invention, meet purpose. By helping Silver define a way his invention could be used, Fry was instrumental in Post-it Notes making their way out of the laboratory and into the marketplace.

> To frame an idea and give it purpose, you don't need to spend a lot of time and resources conducting extensive research.

You don't even need to be lucky enough to have a colleague like Fry who knows precisely what to do with the idea under consideration. Instead, you can make great progress by simply stopping and asking a series of questions.

One useful tool we like to use is the "Five Whys" methodology, originally developed in the 1930s by Sakichi Toyoda, of Toyota Industries (and still used by Toyota today!). The method involves asking why something is important, and then asking why the answer is important, and then asking why that answer is important, and so on. The objective is to achieve more clarity with each subsequent answer to "Why?" The exercise below gives you a firsthand look at how to implement this tool.

Exercise

Articulating Purpose by asking "Why?"

Let's say someone on your team proposes a merger between the sales and marketing groups. You're tempted to discard the idea out of hand. Why would you want to get into the middle of all the internal politics a merger would involve—sorting out who would report to whom and whose job might not be needed anymore? Let's find out why by exploring what the purpose of the merger might be and how it might impact the health of your business.

Step 1

Ask, "**WHY** should sales and marketing merge?"

Answer: Merging would bring together two groups that need to work more closely together.

Step 2

Ask, "**WHY** is it important for the two organizations to work more closely together?"

Answer: If they don't work together, the company can miss marketplace opportunities that could boost revenues and help us take market share from our competitors.

Step 3

Ask, "**WHY** would the company miss marketplace opportunities?"

Answer: The goals of sales and marketing are often disconnected. Sales teams aren't selling the products marketing is promoting. Marketing isn't promoting new products that potential clients tell our sales teams they need.

Step 4

Ask, "WHY are they disconnected?"

Answer: There are no natural communication channels that allow the two separate groups to collaborate and share information freely.

Step 5

Ask, "WHY are there no natural communication channels?"

Answer: With separate groups, reporting structures, goals, and roadmaps for the year, neither group has the power or the incentive to make collaboration happen.

In just five questions, we've gotten to the core purpose of the merger and understand the impact it might have on the broader organization. By using "Why?" to probe further on the answer to each question, you've gone from "Why would anyone want to do this?" to defining the problem you are solving and clarifying some of the key problems the idea might solve. In just a few short steps, you've given the idea "legs." You've reduced the ambiguity and have turned the idea into something that you and others might be more comfortable pursuing further. It's simply a matter of asking "Why?"

Think about an idea you've recently encountered that you might have initially discarded. Try exploring it in new ways using the "Five Whys" process. Use each of the five sets of questions and answers to flesh out the idea further and to define a meaningful purpose it might serve.

Tip 4

Use the POINt Technique

To further evaluate a new idea, we recommend a simple but powerful technique, originally created by Bob Moore at Pfizer, called POINt:

- **P**luses
- **O**pportunities
- **I**ssues
- **N**ew thinking

POINt is designed to help you give each new idea a fair evaluation and to overcome any issues or problems you might discover. It's a strategy you can use by yourself or with a team. You can even use it proactively to establish an effective rationale before you try selling a new idea of your own to others.

Here's how POINt works:

Start with the pluses. Praise the idea. What's good about it and works right now, just as it was presented? Look for the value and articulate the important kernels of the idea that should be kept intact as the idea evolves.

Consider the opportunities. Look at what the future might look like if you implement the idea. What good things might result? What benefits might be uncovered? As you consider the opportunities, start them with the phrase, "It might…." For example, "It might be easier for our customers to reach us if we use this new idea to revamp our customer service process."

Take a clear-eyed look at the issues. No idea is perfect. Rather than killing the idea, though, examine the issues or the limitations that might keep the idea from being a huge success. Phrase the issues as questions that invite a solution. "How will we…?" or "In what ways might we…?"

Declarative statements like "It's too expensive." can shut down a conversation. Focus instead on how to move forward. Ask "How might we reduce the cost?," "In what ways might we get funding?," or "How can we make this initiative work within our existing budget?" "Might" is again the important word here, as it keeps you and everyone focused on possibilities, rather than feasibility.

Use new thinking to overcome issues. Once you've articulated the most important issues that might impede the success of the new idea, spend a little time doing some thinking about solutions. How might the issues be overcome? If the biggest issue is to get funding, for example, spend some time generating ideas to answer that specific question.

If you find yourself pressed for time, keep in mind that you can try a PINt instead of POINt. And if you are *really* short on time, just go with the PI. The main idea is to hold off on judgmental or dismissive comments that can kill a new idea outright. Instead, embrace the ambiguity and uncertainty as you start to nurture ideas that are new and different. When you do, you'll see innovation begin to take on new life in your organization.

Exercise

The POINt Technique in Action

Imagine someone comes to you with an idea for a radical new vending machine. Put money in the coin slot and your dog gets washed and dried. What would your first reaction be? What comments would you make? Write down your first 10 to 12 responses.

Now, look at what you've written. Did you see the potential in this new idea? Or did you focus on the challenges? How might your reaction be different if you used the four-step POINt technique? Review your responses, and attempt to translate them into the POINt structure.

Here are a few ideas to get you started.

- **Consider the pluses of the pet-washing vending machine.** Pet care is a booming industry. Many people hate the mess involved with washing a pet at home.

- **Consider the new opportunities it might open up.** Perhaps you could launch a new line of pet-cleaning products.

- **Consider the issues.** How will you ensure the safety of the pet while it is being washed and dried? How will you keep the machine clean and free of pet hair?

- **Do some "new thinking" about the pet-washing vending machine.** Consider how you might overcome the issues you've identified. Could you add an emergency stop button? Is there a post-wash cycle you could add to clean the machine between uses?

Tip 5
Connect Ideas to Ideas

Not every idea turns out to be useful or actionable on its own. Sometimes you can create great ideas by combining two concepts that were previously unconnected and perhaps unable to stand on their own. While occasionally the combination of two ideas is a matter of happenstance, more often it is the result of deliberately exploring whether you can strengthen an idea by connecting it to other ideas that you've encountered or are able to generate.

Consider what happened when Sony first introduced the Walkman— the first portable device for playing prerecorded music stored on cassette tapes. It was a unique idea that transformed consumer electronics. For the first time you could take your favorite music with you wherever you traveled. The Walkman was so popular that Sony built on the initial idea through the years by merging it with fresh new ideas that solved problems or leveraged opportunities. When cassette tapes became obsolete, Sony built the Walkman with a miniature CD player. When CDs were overtaken by music offered in an MP3 digital format, Sony launched an MP3 player under the Walkman brand.

The cell phone followed a similar innovation path, with new ideas building on new ideas. Martin Cooper and his team at Motorola came up with the idea for a cell phone and made the world's first mobile phone call. The company later brought the idea to market as the DynaTAC, the first commercially available cell phone. IBM built on the idea with a cell phone that could do more than make and receive calls. The company's Simon Personal Communicator was a pricey device that could be used as a pager or to send and receive email and faxes, take notes, schedule appointments, and update calendar entries.

Soon the innovations began to snowball. At the time, cameras and phones had nothing in common. But cell phone manufacturers came up with the idea to merge the two devices into one—giving birth to the selfie generation. The cell phone transformation continues even today, with a seemingly endless combination of new features and apps introduced to keep us interested and eager to purchase the latest model.

The Power of Forced Connections

You can use brainstorming, mind-mapping, and other techniques to help link ideas to ideas. But one of our favorite techniques is something called "forced connections." It's a concept introduced by authors Don Koberg and Jim Bagnall in their book *The Universal Traveler* as a tool for combining seemingly unrelated ideas or attributes to create something new.

Koberg and Bagnall use the ballpoint pen as an example. What if you took a long, cylindrical pen and looked for forced connections to an entirely different shape? Could you create a pen within a cube shape, with one corner of the cube used to expose the tip of a writing cartridge? Could the six faces of the cube then be used for ads or family photos you might want to display on your desk?

When you begin to link together things that, on the surface, have nothing in common, you may actually begin to broaden your perspective and see the initial idea in new, unusual, and highly innovative ways.

Exercise

Connecting Unrelated Ideas

Great ideas frequently come when you combine two things that were previously unconnected. Try making these "forced connections" part of your working process as you and your team evaluate new ideas you encounter. Use the following tips and questions as your guide:

- Select a stimulus or series of stimuli totally unrelated to the original idea you are considering. Perhaps it is a random object, picture, word, physical characteristic, color, or other trait.

- Brainstorm ways you might link these random notions to the problem or opportunity the original idea was intended to address.

- What new associations can you make?

- What new ideas do you get for solving the challenge or making the most of the new opportunity?

- Can you combine any of the new ideas you've generated with the old idea to create something stronger and better?

Here's an example of how the "forced connections" strategy might work. Suppose you are presented with the idea of creating a new beverage product for health-minded consumers. Let's connect the idea to four totally unrelated stimuli—trees, a wheelbarrow, tic-tac-toe, and tigers—to see what kind of new thinking the connections might provoke.

- **New Beverage + Trees.** Some fruits grow on trees. Could you produce a fruit-based beverage packed with Vitamin C and other fruit-based vitamins, but with less sugar and calories than juice?

- **New Beverage + Tiger.** Tigers are fast and energetic— able to run at speeds of 30 to 40 miles per hour in short bursts. Could you produce a low-calorie beverage that gives the consumer a healthy, caffeine-free boost of energy?

- **New Beverage + Wheelbarrow.** A wheelbarrow is designed to help you carry heavy items more easily. Could you create a healthy beverage that includes the amino acids your body needs to protect and build muscle so you can carry weight more effortlessly, just as if you were using a wheelbarrow?

- **New Beverage + Tic-Tac-Toe.** Could the ubiquitous 3 x 3 game grid used to play tic-tac-toe help you generate ideas for packaging your new beverages? Could you offer a "mix and match" three-pack of good-for-you blends—one to build immunity, one to boost energy, and a third to build strength?

Tip 6
Build a Prototype of the Idea

Before you react to a new idea you encounter, it is important that you truly understand what the idea is all about. Each of us has a tendency to believe that people know what we know, see the world in the same way we do, and understand what we are talking about. As a result, when others approach you with a new idea, they may not provide critical clarifying details to reach a level of shared understanding.

One effective strategy is to ask that all new ideas be prototyped so you and others can interact with them and can understand and appreciate what they are about. These preliminary prototype representations of an idea can illustrate how a new product might work or what we mean when we talk about a new concept, process, or service. If you decide the idea has merit and should be pursued further, the prototype can also help you begin to build support for the idea with key stakeholders.

Creating a prototype of an idea should not be time-consuming or costly. It should be something simple that represents the idea and fleshes out some of the specifics so it is more easily communicated. Here are a few examples:

- Create a narrated PowerPoint presentation.
- Fashion a mock-up from found objects.
- Find illustrative photos.
- Draw pictures.
- Create a process flowchart.

29

In many ways, creating the prototype serves as a simple extension of the creativity used to create the idea in the first place. We know a process engineer who had an idea for a better process to sort and refine various powdered chemicals. To help executives understand what he was proposing and why it was important, he drew a diagram depicting the 25 steps in the current process. Beside it he drew a diagram illustrating the significantly fewer steps that the new process he envisioned would entail. Not only did he depict the gist of his new idea, but visually showing the two processes side-by-side easily illustrated why his idea was a good one that could save time and money.

Or consider a beverage industry executive who had the idea for a new soda and took an even simpler approach. His idea was to use light-flavored fruits to add flavors to soda, without overpowering the original soda taste. He chose a photo of a pear and a photo of a bottle of soda and merged the two together as a shorthand prototype of his idea. He didn't go to the time and expense of actually creating a formula for everyone to taste. Instead, his simple visual telegraphed the gist of his idea as he shared it with the team. People were able to quickly "get the picture."

Become an Innovation Hero

Even in organizations that lack a culture where creativity can flourish, individual innovation heroes can emerge. And that hero can be you.

As you become more self-aware and deliberate in how you treat new ideas, you will be poised to make leadership decisions that ripple across your organization.

Your team will become more empowered and engaged. Together you can create and nurture creative new ideas and transform them into new processes, new products, or new services. And you can do it even when there are no or few internal support systems to promote and support innovation.

With this book's six simple tips, you have important building blocks you can practice and use to further your organization's innovation efforts. We hope you get started today. Who knows what great ideas may come your way!

Background

How to Treat New Ideas grew out of CCL's long history of research on creativity, innovation, and helping leaders succeed. Some of CCL's early work in idea generation and innovation included the Targeted Innovation program, which helped participants define specific problems and focus their innovation efforts on achieving creative yet practical solutions. CCL has also done work in exploring the concept of practical creativity in *Making Creativity Practical: Innovation That Gets Results* (Gryskiewicz & Taylor, 2003). Practical creativity aims to produce high-quality ideas which organizations can implement with less risk, providing leaders with another tool to further their innovation efforts.

CCL's current innovation efforts include the Driving Results through Innovation Leadership program, which helps participants drive ideas to implementation while navigating the roadblocks, detours, and challenges which prevent innovative ideas from succeeding in organizations.

Suggested Resources

Gentry, W. A. (2016). *Be the boss everyone wants to work for: A guide for new leaders.* Oakland, CA: Berrett-Koehler Publishers, Inc.

Gryskiewicz, S., & Taylor, S. (2003). *Making creativity practical: Innovation that gets results.* Greensboro, NC: Center for Creative Leadership.

Hallenbeck, G., & CCL Associates. (2017). *Lead 4 success: Learn the essentials of true leadership.* Greensboro, NC: Center for Creative Leadership.

Hallenbeck, G. (2016). *Learning agility: Unlock the lessons of experience.* Greensboro, NC: Center for Creative Leadership.

Horth, D. M., & Vehar., J. (2016). From innovation graveyard to innovation hotbed. *Developing Leaders Quarterly, 23*, 10-16.

Pasmore, B. (2015). *Leading continuous change: Navigating churn in the real world.* Oakland, CA: Berrett-Koehler Publishers, Inc.

Scharlatt, H. (2008). *Selling your ideas to your organization.* Greensboro, NC: Center for Creative Leadership.

About the Center for Creative Leadership

The Center for Creative Leadership (CCL) is a top-ranked, global provider of leadership development. By leveraging the power of leadership to drive results that matter most to clients, CCL transforms individual leaders, teams, organizations, and society. Our array of cutting-edge solutions is steeped in extensive research and experience gained from working with hundreds of thousands of leaders at all levels. Ranked among the world's Top 5 providers of executive education by *Financial Times* and in the Top 10 by *Bloomberg BusinessWeek*, CCL has offices in Greensboro, NC; Colorado Springs, CO; San Diego, CA; Brussels, Belgium; Moscow, Russia; Addis Ababa, Ethiopia; Johannesburg, South Africa; Singapore; Gurgaon, India; and Shanghai, China.

Center for
Creative
Leadership·

IDEAS
INTO
ACTION

Ordering Information

To get more information, to order other books in the Ideas Into Action Series, or to find out about bulk-order discounts, please contact us by phone at 336-545-2810 or visit our online bookstore at www.ccl.org/books.